# Race Around the WORLD

## PATHFINDER EDITION

By Brian LaFleur and Beth Geiger

## CONTENTS

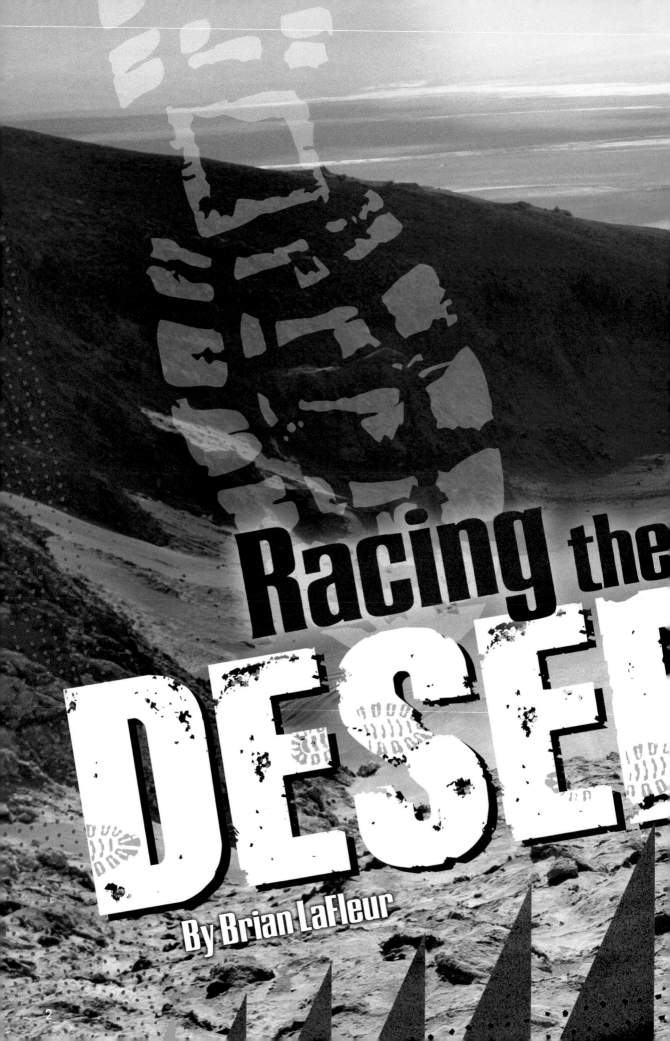

# Racing the DESERT

## By Brian LaFleur

How would you like to race across a brutally hot desert? You will carry all your food and clothes on your back. At the end of the day, you'll be exhausted and collapse in a tent. Then you will wake up the next morning and do it all over again!

Every year, a group of **tough** runners races through the desert. It's not easy, and many of these racers will tell you it's pretty miserable. Yet they do it anyway because they love the challenge.

The runners race across the **harshest** places on Earth. It's all part of the Four Deserts Race. This is no ordinary race. The race has four parts. Each part takes place in a different desert—the Atacama, Gobi, Sahara, and Antarctica. Racers run through the driest, hottest, coldest, and windiest places on Earth!

Each of the parts is 250 kilometers (155 miles) long. Racers must run it in six days. Is this race for you? If so, here's what you need to know.

**Harsh Conditions.** *An Italian racer makes his way across the Atacama Desert in Chile, South America.*

## Desert Data

Before you begin racing, you need to know a bit about deserts. This will help you plan for what you are getting into! Deserts are on every continent. They all have one thing in common—they are dry. Deserts get less than 25 centimeters (10 inches) of rain or snow per year.

That's where the similarities end. You can find deserts in all shapes and sizes. Some deserts are hot and sandy, while others are cold and rocky. Some are flat, and others have mountains. Each desert is different.

These differences mean that each desert has its own challenges for the racers. You'll be hot one week, and cold the next. You'll climb mountains and trudge through sand.

## The Dry Atacama

So you've studied up on deserts, and you're ready for the race. You've trained for months. You've packed your clothes and your food. Let the race begin!

In March, you fly to Chile, in South America. Here, you face the Atacama—the first desert in the race. It is also the driest place on Earth. Scientists have measured rainfall here a long time. In some places, not one drop of water has ever been seen! The land is so **desolate** and dry that people came here to make movies about Mars!

The worst part of this race is the salt plains. None of your training can prepare you for this. One racer said it was like "stepping on millions of pieces of broken glass, uneven pebbles, and hard rocks at the same time."

When you reach the finish line, you may forget the pain. Do you want to do it all over again? Good—because you still have three more deserts to cross!

## Four Deserts Race Locations

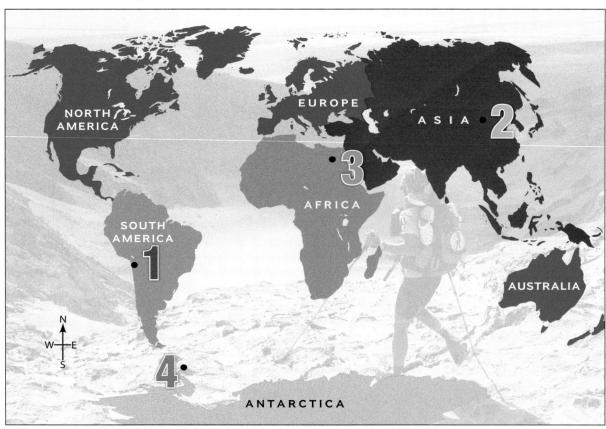

# 1  Atacama Desert

**Driest Desert.** *Llamas rest in Chile's Atacama Desert.*

## Extreme Gobi

After Chile, you have some time to head home and rest. In June, it's time to race again! For this part, you fly to China where you'll tackle the Gobi. It has some sandy areas, but most of the Gobi is rocky.

It is tough to pack for this part of the race. The Gobi is a place of **extremes**. Burning hot days can turn to freezing cold nights. It may be summertime, but in the mountains you face strong winds and even snow. It's best to pack layers that you can put on and peel off.

You may meet some people as you run the Gobi. Many of the people who live here are nomads. Nomads move from place to place, and many of them herd camels, sheep, or goats. They move to wherever there is food and water for their animals. You have to keep moving, too! Soon, you'll be halfway done with the race.

# 2  Gobi

**Desert Delivery.** *For centuries, camels have carried people and goods across the Gobi in China.*

**3 Sahara**

**Fierce Wind.** *In Egypt, wind carved the rock and blew the sand of this Sahara landscape.*

## The Singing Sahara

In October, you travel to the Sahara in North Africa. It is the hottest place on Earth. Heat is not the only challenge. You shuffle through sand, sand, and more sand. Fierce winds often whip the sand around. This can create strong sandstorms. Racers cover their faces to breathe.

Still, the sand isn't all bad. Sometimes, it has a beautiful sound, called singing sand. It can sound like a squeal, a hum, or a roar. Not all deserts have singing sands. Luckily, you're racing through one that does!

Even after a week, you have seen only a bit of this desert. The Sahara is Earth's biggest hot desert. And it's growing. Droughts and overfarming can cause deserts to grow. Dry land creeps into areas that were once green. This process is called desertification.

## Icy Antarctica

After you cross the Sahara, it's time for the last part of the race. It may also be the hardest. Only racers who finish other parts of the race can tackle this desert. You're heading to Antarctica. That's right—Antarctica is a desert!

It is the coldest and windiest place on Earth, and parts of this icy continent get less than five centimeters (two inches) of moisture per year. Though not much snow falls, it piles up for centuries in the extreme cold. Winds here can reach speeds of 300 kilometers (186 miles) per hour.

As you move through knee-deep snow, you won't be alone. Hundreds of curious birds like gentoo and chinstrap penguins watch you. Other birds spy on you from above, and seals splash around nearby. They may help you forget how tired your body is!

## End in Sight

With extreme **effort**, the end of the race is in sight. You push yourself over the finish line in Antarctica. It is the last one. Congratulations! The Four Deserts Race is over. You made it.

As you think about the amazing things you saw, you forget all your aches, blisters, and sunburns. After all, these deserts may be the harshest places on Earth, but they are also some of the most beautiful.

**Almost There.** *Congratulations! You finished the third race! One more to go!*

## Wordwise

**desolate:** empty, without people

**effort:** hard work to do something

**extreme:** a very great degree of something

**harsh:** hard and unpleasant

**tough:** strong and determined; difficult to do

Antarctica

**Icy Cold.** *Surrounding the South Pole, Antarctica is Earth's coldest continent.*

# EXTREMES

*By Beth Geiger*

Earth is full of extremes, and you are invited to explore them. You can climb the highest peak, sail down the greatest river, shiver on the coldest continent, and more.

Great
Barrier
Reef

**AUSTRALIA**

**Coral Kingdom.** Tiny sea creatures called coral polyps built a huge, stony structure off the coast of Australia. It is called the Great Barrier Reef. Largest of all coral reefs, it is 2,000 kilometers (1,250 miles) long.

**Enormous Everest.**
No peak stands taller than Mount Everest. It lies on the border of China and Nepal. The top is 8,850 meters (29,035 feet) high.

ASIA
←Mt. Everest

Sahara

AFRICA

**Sizzling Sands.** The Sahara is the largest hot desert on Earth. Stretching across northern Africa, it is about the size of the United States. Some parts get no rain for years at a time.

**Coldest Continent.**
Thick ice blankets Antarctica, the land surrounding the South Pole. Even in the summer, temperatures generally stay below freezing.

ANTARCTICA

NORTH AMERICA

Grand Canyon

**The Grandest Canyon.**
Carved by the Colorado River, the Grand Canyon snakes its way through northwestern Arizona. The canyon is 446 kilometers (227 miles) long.

**Fantastic Falls.**
Angel Falls is Earth's tallest waterfall. It is in Venezuela. Water plunges 970 meters (3,212 feet) from the top of a cliff.

Angel Falls

**SOUTH AMERICA**

Amazon River

**SOUTH AMERICA**

**Awesome Amazon.**
No river carries more water than the Amazon. It flows east across Brazil. Around this mighty river stands the world's largest rain forest.

# AROUND EARTH

**Explore the most extreme places on the planet to answer these questions.**

**1** What is the Four Deserts Race? Where does it take place?

**2** Why are deserts such extreme places?

**3** How is each desert different from the others?

**4** What can you learn about each desert from the photos on pages 4–7?

**5** How are deserts like other extreme places on Earth? How are they different?